A NOTE TO PARENTS

When your children are ready to "step into reading," giving them the right books is as crucial as giving them the right food to eat. **Step into Reading Books** present exciting stories and information reinforced with lively, colorful illustrations that make learning to read fun, satisfying, and worthwhile. They are priced so that acquiring an entire library of them is affordable. And they are beginning readers with a difference—they're written on five levels.

Early Step into Reading Books are designed for brand-new readers, with large type and only one or two lines of very simple text per page. **Step 1 Books** feature the same easy-to-read type as the Early Step into Reading Books, but with more words per page. **Step 2 Books** are both longer and slightly more difficult, while **Step 3 Books** introduce readers to paragraphs and fully developed plot lines. **Step 4 Books** offer exciting nonfiction for the increasingly independent reader.

The grade levels assigned to the five steps—preschool through kindergarten for the Early Books, preschool through grade 1 for Step 1, grades 1 through 3 for Step 2, grades 2 through 3 for Step 3, and grades 2 through 4 for Step 4—are intended only as guides. Some children move through all five steps very rapidly; others climb the steps over a period of several years. Either way, these books will help your child "step into reading" in style!

Thanks to Dr. Paul G. Bahn
for his assistance in the preparation of this book.

Cover Photographs: R. M. Arakaki/International Stock; Paul Hanny/Gamma Liaison.
Interior Photographs: page 43 by J. C. Aunos/Gamma Liaison; page 43 by K.
Bernstein/Spooner/Gamma Liaison; pages 4 and 33 by Steve Casimiro/Gamma Liaison;
pages 20, 21, 22, 23 and 24 by Gamma Liason; page 35 by Kenneth Garrett/National
Geographic Magazine; pages 41 and 47 by Grossruck/Contrast/Gamma Liaison; pages 9,
10, 11, and 28 by Paul Hanny/Gamma Liaison; pages 27 and 30 by Gerhand
Hinterleitner/Gamma Liaison; page 45 by M. C. R. Communications/Gamma Liaison; page
39 by Dave Nagel/Gamma Liaison; pages 6, 7, 15, 16, 17, 29, 31, and 35 by Sygma; pages
36 and 48 by Zefiro & Luna/Gamma Liaison;

www.randomhouse.com/kids
Library of Congress Cataloging-in-Publication Data
Dubowski, Cathy East.
Ice mummy : The discovery of a 5,000-year-old man / by Cathy Dubowski and Mark
Dubowski ; illustrated with photographs. p. cm. (Step into Reading. A step 3 book)
SUMMARY: Describes the discovery by Alpine hikers near the Austrian-Italian border of
the frozen body of a man who, after careful examination, was found to be more than
5,000 years old.
ISBN 0-679-85647-1 (pbk.) — ISBN 0-679-95647-6 (lib. bdg.).
1. Copper age—Italy—Hauslobjoch Pass—Juvenile literature.
2. Mummies—Italy—Hauslobjoch Pass—Juvenile literature.
3. Hauslobjoch Pass (Italy)—Antiquities—Juvenile literature.
[1. Prehistoric peoples. 2. Mummies. 3. Copper age. 4. Excavations (Archaeology)]
I. Dubowski, Mark. II. Title. III. Series: Step into reading. Step 3 book.
GN778.2.I8D82 1998 937—dc21 97-30998

Printed in the United States of America 10 9 8 7 6 5

STEP INTO READING is a registered trademark of Random House, Inc.

Step into Reading®

Ice Mummy

The Discovery of a 5,000-Year-Old Man

by Mark Dubowski
and Cathy East Dubowski
—With photographs—

A Step 3 Book

Random House 🏠 New York

Chapter 1

AN AMAZING DISCOVERY

It is September 19, 1991, a bright, sunny day.

German tourists Helmut and Erika Simon are hiking in snow-covered mountains. The mountains are called the Alps. The Simons are near the border where Austria meets Italy.

They have hiked here many times before. There is usually snow on the ground, even in the summer. But this year the weather has been warm. There is not as much snow as usual.

Suddenly Erika sees something odd sticking up in the snow. What could it be? At first Helmut thinks it is a doll's head.

He is wrong.

"It's a man!" cries Erika.

The man lies facedown, half buried in the ice. The Simons look closely.

The man is dead.

Was he a hiker? they wonder. Did he get lost in a storm? Did someone kill him?

Quickly they take a photograph of the body. Then they hurry to the next hikers'

The Ice Mummy, as he was found.

shelter to report their discovery.

The man who runs the shelter calls the police right away.

The Alps can be dangerous. The trails are rocky and steep. Fast-moving storms can catch hikers off guard. Sometimes hikers die. The police are called to bring out the bodies.

He lay facedown in the melting snow.

7

The police are very busy. They cannot come that day. They cannot come the next day, either. The man who runs the shelter decides to hike up the mountain to see the body for himself.

How strange! the man thinks. He has seen people frozen in the ice before. Their skin always looks white and waxy. But the skin of this body is brown and dry.

That's not all. Broken pieces of carved wood are scattered around the body.

And the body is dressed in clothing made of animal skins.

It gives the man from the shelter an odd feeling. This body must be very old.

How old?

He thinks it might be a hundred years old…

He had been deeply frozen in the thick ice.

Two days later a helicopter lands in the snow. A police officer gets out.

He sees the body frozen deep in the ice. The officer tries to break it free with a jackhammer.

Tat-at-at-at!

The jackhammer stabs into the ice. It hits the body, strikes a bone, then runs out of power.

The police officer cannot go back for more tools now. The helicopter is needed for other business. He says he will come back in a few days.

Word spreads about the strange body frozen in the ice. Over the next two days, many hikers go to see it. The man from the shelter covers the body with a blanket to keep them away.

But they don't stay away. Some people try to dig the body out of the ice. They

take pictures of it. They even tear scraps of clothing from the body as souvenirs.

A famous mountain climber comes by to take a look. His name is Reinhold Messner. He does not touch or take things.

Mountain climbers come to take a look.

He looks carefully at the body. It wears a cape made of woven grass. The carved sticks around the body look to him like pieces of tools.

Reinhold Messner does not think the body is a hundred years old.

He thinks it may be *thousands* of years old!

Chapter 2

OUT OF THE ICE

The police phone an expert for help. Dr. Rainer Henn agrees to come.

Dr. Henn's job is to examine dead bodies and figure out how they died. He is called a medical examiner.

The police want him to figure out what happened to the man in the ice.

Dr. Henn takes a helicopter to the mountaintop. After one look at the body, he knows that this is a big discovery!

Dr. Henn has seen many dead bodies before. Hundreds. But he has never seen one like this.

It's a *mummy!*

Dr. Rainer Henn carefully turning the Iceman over.

Dr. Henn knows the mummy must be moved very carefully. But he does not have the right tools to get it out of the ice. Should he leave and come back later?

No. He does not want to leave the mummy in the open any longer. People or animals may do it more harm.

Dr. Henn and assistant carefully remove the mummy from the ice.

So Dr. Henn borrows an ax and a ski pole from a hiker. He chops at the ice around the body.

It's hard work. But finally he drags the mummy out.

Around its waist is a kind of tool belt. On the belt is a small knife with a wooden handle. But it is not a modern knife with a steel blade.

This blade is made of stone!

Dr. Henn and his helpers put the mummy in a body bag. They pick up everything they find around the site. The carved wood. An ax. They put it all in the helicopter. Then they fly to the nearest village.

The Iceman being transported to a nearby village.

There, they put the mummy in a coffin. Then they put the coffin in a long black car. It looks as if they are going to a funeral!

But they do not drive the mummy to a graveyard to be buried.

The Iceman is placed into a coffin.

They take the mummy to the medical school where Dr. Henn works.

Dr. Henn asks other scientists to look at it. No one has ever seen *anything* like this.

Meanwhile, people all over the world are talking about the frozen mummy. Who

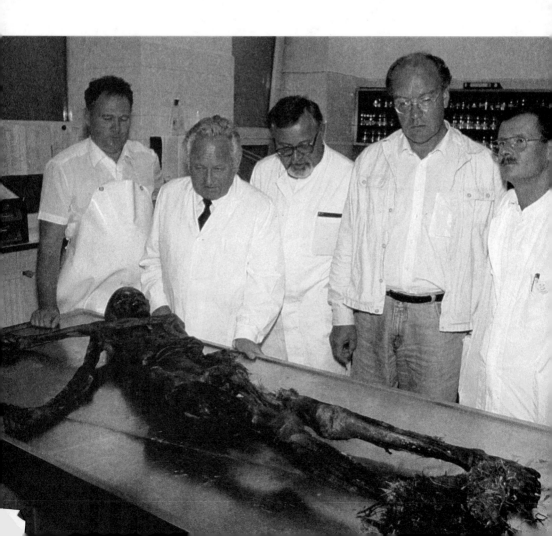

was he? Where is he being kept? What's the big secret?

Dr. Henn's phone rings off the hook. Newspapers, magazines, and television stations all over the world want to talk to him.

They all want to break the Ice Mummy story!

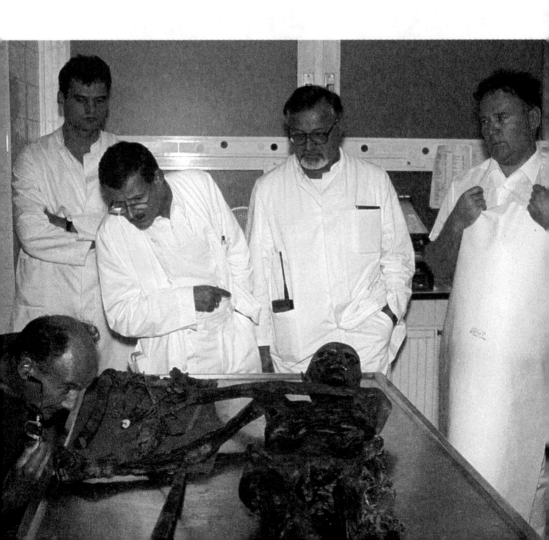

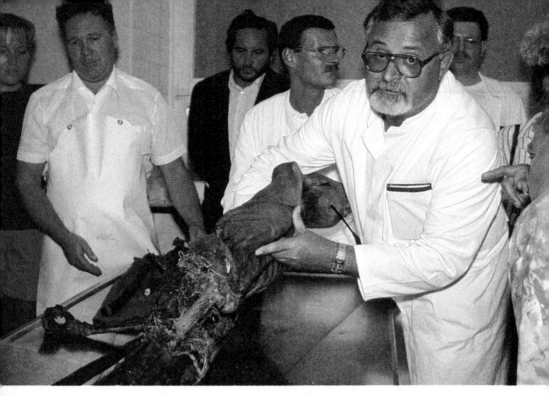
Reporters crowd Dr. Henn and his team.

Flash!

Reporters crowd around, snapping pictures.

Dr. Henn has invited them to the medical school where he works to have a look at the mummy.

The reporters give it a nickname: the Iceman. They poke at the mummy.

One TV reporter gets an idea for a joke. He hides behind the mummy. Then he makes its hand wave to the camera.

Things are getting out of control.

Meanwhile, something is happening to the mummy. At first everyone is too busy to notice. Then someone points.

"Look!" Something is growing on the mummy's skin.

It looks as if mold is spreading all over his body!

The Iceman is thawing out!

After just a few days around people, flashbulbs, and television lights, the mummy is starting to rot!

The scientists act quickly. First, they wash the Iceman with a hospital germ-killer.

A scientist carefully washes the mummy.

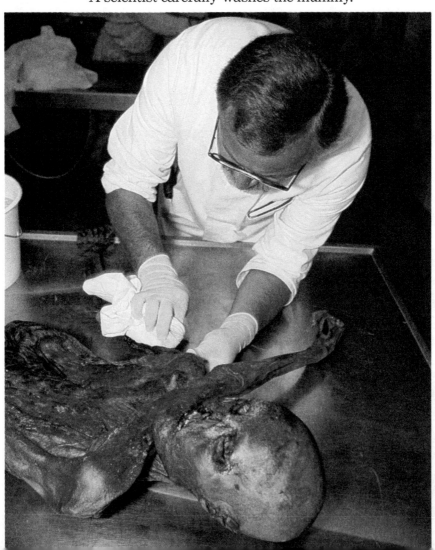

Then they put him in a cold room. It is like a big refrigerator.

Inside the room it is 21.2 degrees Fahrenheit—the same temperature as the ice.

Kept cold in this room, the mummy is safe from rotting.

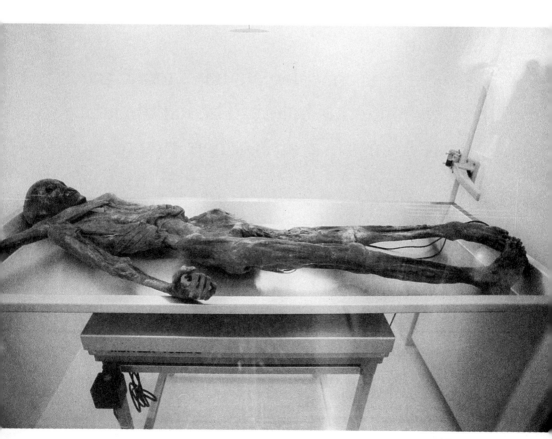

He lay safely in a refrigerated room.

Finally the mummy is examined by an archaeologist (ar-kee-AHL-uh-jist)—an expert in ancient people. He is Dr. Konrad Spindler.

Dr. Spindler enters the cold room. He looks closely at the body.

He looks at the knife with the stone blade.

But most of all, he looks at the Iceman's ax.

Other archaeologists have found parts of axes like this before. The handle is made from a tree limb, where two branches grew apart. A blade is wrapped in place where the branches forked. The blade is made of copper.

Experts know that axes like this were used by people thousands of years ago.

Dr. Spindler says this ax tells us that the Iceman is at least 4,000 years old!

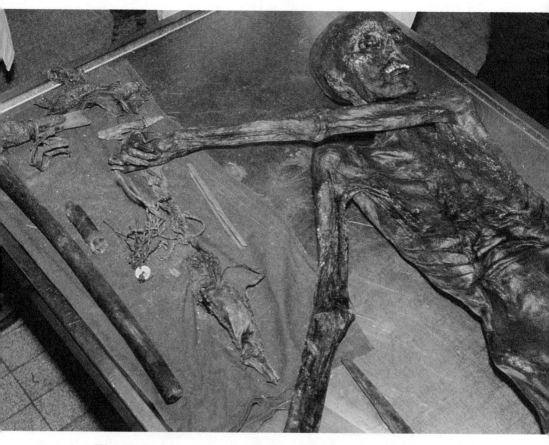

The Iceman's tools are neatly arranged beside him.

Scientists all over the world want to know more. They ask many questions.

Where was he found? What was he wearing? What things were found with him?

They are like detectives trying to solve a mystery. Here is the evidence:

His Body

We know that the Iceman was found facedown on the ground. We also know that he did not die from an injury or sickness. He was about thirty years old when he died. What killed him?

The scientists think he froze to death during a storm.

He was still wearing one grass shoe.

His Clothing

The Iceman was wearing a jacket, pants, and boots made of animal skins. The sewing was expertly done—except where rips were fixed with rough stitches, probably made while out on the trail.

This makes scientists think he came from a village where the clothes were made by skilled hands.

His Tools

We know the Iceman carried a back-pack, a bow and arrows, a net that could be used to catch fish or birds, and an ax.

Because of this, scientists think he was camping in the mountains.

A box made of tree bark was found near the Iceman's hand. Inside were pieces of burned wood. Coals. Probably from his campfires.

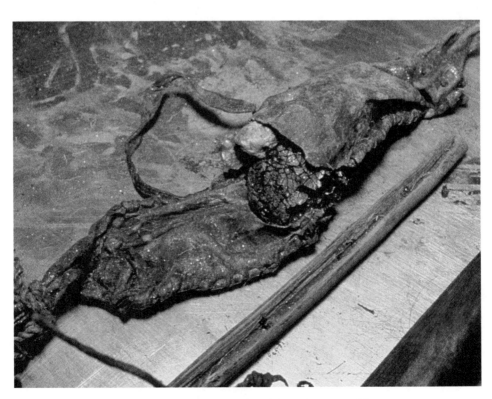

The Iceman's backpack with arrows and bow.

Some of the coals are from wood that grows high up the mountain. Other coals in the same box are from wood that only grows in the valleys.

The Iceman's ax, knife, and other tools.

From this, scientists think he made many campfires in many different places. He was probably a long way from home when he died.

The experts agree about some things. Others they are not so sure about. The big mystery is how the Iceman became a mummy. How could his body have dried out under the snow and ice?

Normally the Alps are very cold throughout the year. Even in summer. But once in a while, the weather is not so cold.

Some scientists think warm wind blew snow off the body and dried it out, turning it into a mummy.

Others say the body would not have lasted if it was uncovered at any time. They say that birds or other animals would have destroyed it.

These experts think the body stayed under the snow and ice the whole time. They think that if the snow and ice were frozen very hard, moisture could evaporate from the body.

A scientific test called carbon-14 dating can tell the age of almost anything that ever lived—dead animals, dead people, plants, or things like cloth, which comes from living matter.

How old is the Ice Mummy? Carbon-14 dating shows he is more than 5,000 years old!

Getting to know the Ice Mummy better is not just a job for scientists. Artists work from a model of the Iceman's skull to sculpt what his face might have looked like.

The mummy is in such good condition that we know for sure he had blue eyes, a gap between his front teeth, and a neat haircut. He was five feet two and weighed 110 pounds. He wore an earring in his right ear and had tattoos on his back, legs, and feet.

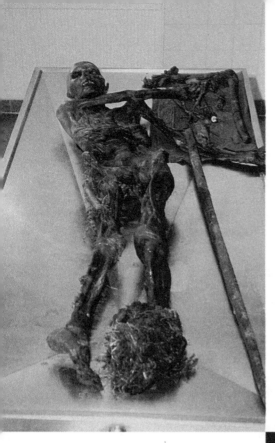

Laid out with his tools and his walking stick, the Iceman has much to teach scientists and archaelogists.

Using x-ray photos and moldings, artist John Gurche was able to reconstruct the Ice Mummy's face.

Chapter 3

HIS LAST DAY

It is the year 3000 B.C. It is almost winter.

The high mountain trail is clear of snow. It is easy to follow.

But not for long. A storm is on the way.

The man on the trail stops. He looks at the sky. He feels the icy wind on his face. This is a bad place to be in a storm. There are no trees to block the wind and no wood to make a fire.

The storm hits. He finds a low place to hide. He hunkers down against the cold.

Far away, in the man's village, people are safe from the storm. They wait it out in log houses. They have fire and food and water.

In one house, children play. Their mother watches over them. On her lap is a jacket made of animal skin. She is sewing neat stitches along one edge.

She wonders about the man in the mountains. He has been away for many days.

She hopes he is in a good place to wait out the storm.

The man in the mountains holds a small box made from damp strips of bark. The box holds a few hot coals from the fire he made the night before.

When the man opens the box, the fresh air makes the coals glow brightly.

Hours pass. The wind howls and snow keeps falling.

The man falls asleep, thinking of home.
The coals burn out.
By morning he has frozen to death and
is covered with a blanket of snow.

The Alps, still deadly today.

Chapter 4

THE ICE MUMMY TODAY

What might the Iceman have called his native land? Today, we call the spot where he died Italy. And that is where the Iceman is today.

A museum was built for him in the city of Bolzano. You can see the mummy there. You can see his things there, too—his clothing, his tools, and his bronze ax.

The Iceman is safe inside a special room. A room with thick walls and bulletproof glass windows. A room that is always—and always will be—cold as ice.

The Ice Mummy's clothing on exhibit in Bolzano, Italy.

Chapter 5

MUMMIES

What exactly is a mummy? A mummy is a body that has been preserved—kept as close as possible to the way it was when it was alive.

The Ice Mummy was preserved by nature. Other mummies have been preserved by people.

Man-made mummies have been found on almost every continent. In ancient Egypt, dead human bodies were dried in sand or soda ash. The bodies were buried in pyramids, along with treasure for use in the next life. In South America, bodies were dried with heat and smoke and buried in baskets or large pottery jars. In North America, bodies were wrapped in

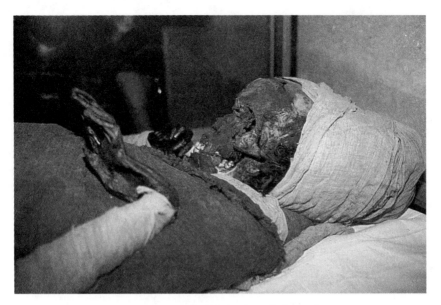

An Egyptian mummy on exhibit in a Cairo, Egypt, museum.

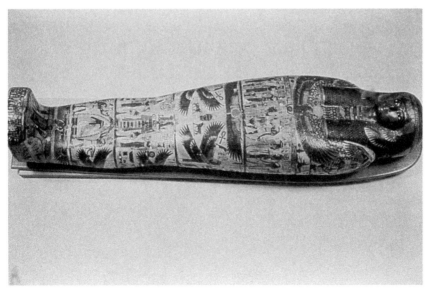

3000-year-old sarcophagus of the priestess Tjentmutenebitu.

leather and stored in caves, where they were preserved by the cold.

Another kind of mummy preserved by nature is found in bogs. Bogs are places where the ground is wet and soft. If you step in the wrong place, you can sink in mud that is very deep.

Bog mummies were not dried for burial. They were not placed carefully in graves with sacred objects. They fell—or were thrown—into bogs and drowned. Because bog mud contains natural germ-killers, the bodies did not rot.

So far, the oldest bog mummies that have been found are about 2,000 years old.

That is old, but not nearly as old as the Ice Mummy!

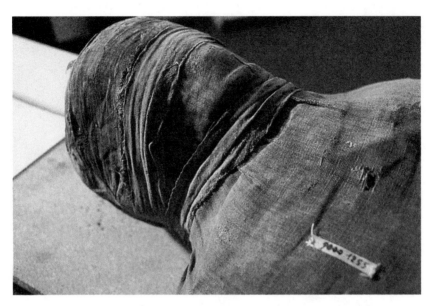

A fully wrapped mummy.

An Egyptian mummy with a ceremonial statue on display in a museum.

Chapter 6

TIME TRAVELER

Helmut and Erika Simon's snapshots of the Iceman are like pictures out of a time machine.

They show an ancient man, unmoved from where he lay down for the last time more than 5,000 years ago.

A man who went walking in the mountains before the mountains were called the Alps.

He shows us the things you would need for a long journey in the year 3000 B.C.

What you would wear.

How you would hunt.

How you would make a fire.

And how life—like a snowstorm—can catch you by surprise.

How the Iceman would have looked more than 5,000 years ago.

Are there others like him out there?
Lost…and waiting to be found?